Skyscrapers

By Virginia Loh-Hagan

21st Century
Junior Library

Published in the United States of America by
Cherry Lake Publishing
Ann Arbor, Michigan
www.cherrylakepublishing.com

Content Adviser: Dr. Todd Kelley, Associate Professor of Engineering/Technology Teacher Education, Purdue Polytechnic Institute, West Lafayette, Indiana
Reading Adviser: Marla Conn MS, Ed., Literacy specialist, Read-Ability, Inc.

Photo Credits: © pisaphotography/Shutterstock Images, cover; © Ronnie Chua/Shutterstock Images, 4; © Javen/Shutterstock Images, 6; © joreks/Shutterstock Images, 8; © pan demin/Shutterstock Images, 10; © Richard Cavalleri/Shutterstock Images, 12; © Pavel Ganchev – Paf/Shutterstock Images, 14; © Anastasios71/Shutterstock Images, 16; © AvDe/Shutterstock Images, 18

Library of Congress Cataloging-in-Publication Data
Names: Loh-Hagan, Virginia, author.
Title: Skyscrapers / by Virginia Loh-Hagan.
Description: Ann Arbor : Cherry Lake Publishing, 2017. | Series: 21st century junior library. Extraordinary engineering | Audience: K to grade 3. | Includes bibliographical references and index.
Identifiers: LCCN 2016032397 | ISBN 9781634721653 (hardcover) | ISBN 9781634722971 (pbk.) | ISBN 9781634722315 (pdf) | ISBN 9781634723633 (ebook)
Subjects: LCSH: Skyscrapers–Juvenile literature. | Skyscrapers–Design and construction–Juvenile literature.
Classification: LCC TH1615 .L64 2017 | DDC 720/.483–dc23
LC record available at https://lccn.loc.gov/2016032397

Cherry Lake Publishing would like to acknowledge the work of The Partnership for 21st Century Learning.
Please visit *www.p21.org* for more information.

Printed in the United States of America
Corporate Graphics

CONTENTS

The city with the most skyscrapers in the world is Hong Kong.

What Are Skyscrapers?

The word **skyscraper** was first used in the 1880s. This is when the first tall buildings were built in the United States. People looked up. These buildings looked like they touched the sky.

Skyscrapers are the world's tallest buildings. They have over 50 **stories**. They stick out from other buildings. They create a city's **skyline**.

The CN Tower in Toronto, Canada, is one of the tallest towers in the world.

Skyscrapers are different from **towers**. Towers are tall. They have thick walls. They don't have windows. Windows weaken buildings. Large numbers of people don't live or work in towers. Towers can be used as military defenses, to support bridges, or as antennas for communication. They don't have much **usable** space inside. Skyscrapers do. They use a small footprint, or ground area. They make space by adding stories. They offer more room this way. Many people live and work in them.

The invention of long steel beams made skyscrapers like the Empire State Building in New York City possible.

How Do Skyscrapers Support Weight?

Originally, buildings were made of only bricks or stone. They were heavy. They couldn't be higher than 10 stories. Then, steel was invented. Steel is lighter and stronger. It supports more weight. Steel allows engineers to design taller buildings.

Skyscrapers have steel **skeletons**. These skeletons support walls. They spread out **load**. Top floors move weight into steel **beams** and down to the **foundation**.

Skyscrapers' center of gravity needs to be
underground in the foundation.

Gravity pulls down skyscrapers. So, all the weight goes to the foundations underground. The ground can hold heavy loads. Some foundations are **anchored** in solid rock. Foundations carry the skeletons' load. Foundations spread out and move the **forces** down to the ground. This supports the combined weight at the top of the building.

Look!

Look at the tallest building in town. How tall is it? How many stories does it have? Look up. Do you think it sways in the wind?

The John Hancock Center in Chicago, Illinois, can sway up to
15 inches (38 centimeters) in strong winds.

How Do Skyscrapers Resist Forces?

Engineers think about forces. Wind and earthquakes can affect skyscrapers. They cause **vibrations**. This makes skyscrapers sway. Skyscrapers can sway a little. They're like trees. They move with vibrations. Engineers design them to do so. This is so skeletons don't get twisted or strained. But skyscrapers can't sway too much. They must resist strong winds.

Engineers break up wind forces.

Engineers design a steel inner **core**. They put poles and beams together. This provides strong support. In newer skyscrapers, engineers design a hollow tube. Engineers move the core support. Poles and beams are placed on outer edges. Skyscrapers can be even taller. Engineers sometimes combine both designs.

Think!

Think about the benefits of skyscrapers. Why are skyscrapers more common in big cities? Why are skyscrapers a good design for big cities?

The elevators in the world's tallest building, the Burj Khalifa in Dubai, travel nearly 2,000 feet (609.6 meters) per second.

How Do Skyscrapers Serve People's Needs?

Imagine getting to the top of skyscrapers. That's a lot of stairs! **Elevators** make skyscrapers possible. They help people get around. They also support skyscrapers. They're built into the inner cores of the buildings. Engineers **brace** elevator **shafts** using steel **trusses**. This gives skyscrapers stronger cores. This also spreads out load.

Elevator shafts take up a lot of space.

Each floor needs elevators. Each floor also needs services. Skyscrapers need hallways and staircases. They need heating, air, and water. Pumps bring water to skyscrapers. Engineers study how these things work. They decide if adding floors is worth it. They decide if skyscrapers can handle the load.

Ask Questions!

Ask friends or family if they've been in a skyscraper. Ask if they went to the top. Some people are scared of heights. Why would skyscrapers scare them?

Try This!

Materials

2 thick pieces of cardboard,
2 rubber bands, ruler, 4 small
rubber balls, large LEGO baseplate,
LEGO bricks

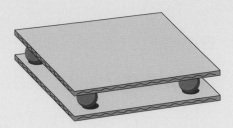

Procedures

1 Stack cardboard pieces together. Wrap rubber bands around ends. Leave 1 inch (2.5 cm) at edges

2 Place balls between cardboard pieces. Place one at each corner. Place balls about 2 inches (5 cm) in from each corner.

3 Put LEGO baseplate on top. Slip it under the rubber bands.

4 Use LEGO bricks to build several LEGO towers. Do this on a nearby surface. Use same base size. Make different heights.

5 Place each tower on the baseplate. Place in center. Do this one at a time.

6 Tug on the top layer of cardboard. Let it go. See what happens to each tower. Does it fall? Does it stay in place?

Principle at Play

This activity shows how tall structures are less stable than shorter ones. Especially in earthquake zones, tall buildings are likely to fall. They need to be supported. Change the base size. Change the height. Change the materials. See what happens.

GLOSSARY

anchored (ANG-kurd) firmly placed in the ground

beams (BEEMZ) long, sturdy pieces of steel used to support buildings

brace (BRASE) to fasten objects together for support

core (KOR) the center

elevators (EL-uh-vay-turz) machines that help people travel up and down buildings

forces (FORS-iz) pushing or pulling motions

foundation (foun-DAY-shuhn) the stable structure on which a building is constructed

gravity (GRAV-ih-tee) force that attracts objects toward the center of the earth

load (LOHD) where weight falls in a building

shafts (SHAFTS) long, narrow passages that go straight down, through which elevators travel

skeletons (SKEL-uh-tuhnz) the frameworks holding up buildings

skyline (SKYE-line) outline of land and buildings defined against the sky

skyscraper (SKYE-skray-pur) tall buildings with over 50 stories

stories (STOR-eez) floors of a building

towers (TOU-urz) tall structures

trusses (TRUHS-iz) support braces using a pattern of triangles

usable (YOOZ-uh-buhl) capable of being used

vibrations (vye-BRAY-shuhnz) movements like tremors

FIND OUT MORE

BOOKS

Latham, Donna, and Andrew Christensen (illustrator). *Skyscrapers: Investigate Feats of Engineering*. White River Junction, VT: Nomad Press, 2013.

Malam, John, and David Antram (illustrator). *You Wouldn't Want to Be a Skyscraper Builder! A Hazardous Job You'd Rather Not Take*. New York: Franklin Watts, 2009.

Price, Sean Stewart. *The Story Behind Skyscrapers*. Chicago: Heinemann, 2009.

Shea, Therese. *How a Skyscraper Is Built*. New York: Gareth Stevens Publishing, 2016.

WEB SITES

HowStuffWorks—How Skyscrapers Work
http://science.howstuffworks.com/engineering/structural/skyscraper.htm
Learn about the innovations that made skyscrapers possible.

PBS—Building Big: Skyscrapers
www.pbs.org/wgbh/buildingbig/skyscraper
Learn the basics about skyscrapers and see examples of them.

INDEX

ABOUT THE AUTHOR

Dr. Virginia Loh-Hagan is an author, university professor, former classroom teacher, and curriculum designer. She has an original painting of the Twin Towers. It's hanging over her fireplace. She lives in San Diego with her very tall husband and very naughty dogs. To learn more about her, visit www.virginialoh.com.